My System - Your System

Budgeting made simple for everyone

Kathleen Walter

Dedications/acknowledgements etc.

I would like to dedicate this book to my lovely daughters, Colleen, Kirsty and Stacey. My grandchildren Jasmine, Schanel, Hunter and future family, whom I hope will take on board My System now that it has been turned into a book to help make life easier.

And my thanks go out to my husband Heinz. He has always given me love and support in anything I have chosen to venture into, usually without question. My sister Judy, brother in-law Richard, sister in-law Barbara, thanks for always listening.

And Melanie Cahani who, without her expertise and friendship gave me the drive, inspiration and encouragement to actually get my system out there or it would still be in the cupboard.

Kathleen May Walter

Contents

I first started my system in 1977 when I separated and became a single mum with one daughter. I then remarried and we had twin daughters.

We have never looked back. We had three children under three and just one income. We could not afford daycare and in any case, daycare as it is known today was not available for most people.

We had 18% interest on our mortgage. Granted a family home only cost around $40,000.00 back then, but remember our incomes were in line with that, so money was just as tight then as it is now.

I grew up in a government house, as we used to call them, and at that time government housing was plentiful but we went ahead and purchased our block of land to build our own home on it.

My husband and I were never very high income earners but my system has allowed us to travel and live a comfortable and fulfilling lifestyle.

My System, Your System
written by
Kathleen-Housewife
AUSTRALIA

My System is designed to help you to organise your incoming bills into a manageable system. It is not within the scope of this book to tell you how to pay off your debts, but it can help. The system is set out in simple and straightforward steps, making it easy for anyone and everyone to follow, and meaning you can easily adjust it to suit the requirements of your own lifestyle and routines.

If you follow all the simple rules, this system will never fail you. In order for My System to successfully become Your System, there must be rules in place. Once you have transformed My System into Your System, you will have peace of mind and you will never need to worry about an unexpected or a large bill ever again.

My System is for everyday household budgeting, not for helping you to get out of debt, but if you apply this system carefully and follow the guidelines, you will find it easier to get on top of your debts and may even be able to pay them off more quickly. Using My System all the time will help you to stay out of debt.

My System is not just for those on a large income or with a large amount of money left over every pay-period. Neither is it just for low-income households. It is designed for anyone who wants to gain a greater control over their budget, to keeping spending habits controlled and who want to know where their money is going every pay-period. It is about how you can manage your income and make it work to your advantage.

It will take the worry out of every incoming bill that you will receive over a 12-month period. Imagine how you will feel when the next amount is due and you have your payment ready! This will be possible when you put into practise My

System's rules and by doing so, you will turn it into Your System. You will have an account on paper for everything you need to save for.

Follow The Rules

My System works better and much more efficiently if you itemise your bills to every payday whether that is weekly, fortnightly or monthly. This way, it will show you the exact balance you are holding for any particular bill.

One important point to keep in mind - you cannot take money from any of your bills and pay back later. You must promise not to touch any amounts that belong to another bill and stick with that promise. In other words, remember the old saying, 'you cannot rob Peter to pay Paul'.

We will file our bills in a folder and we will be using subdividers to separate each bill into its own section under its appropriate name. You can add any item to your system. It does not have to be a bill as such, it may be something you want to save towards. You may want to take holidays so if you can afford it you can allow for this in Your System.

In the same way, you may want to save for a new car, a new kitchen, a college fund for your kids, you might be planning a wedding. Anything that is important to you and will require funds, you can save for using this system, simply by building it into your everyday budget.

If you find it easier or more convenient, you can create a spreadsheet that will do the same job as a folder and subdividers! But it is essential to ensure you calculate your budgeting to fit within your income.

If you cannot afford what Your System is doing for you, go back over your bills, as you may have to adjust where necessary. And don't plan to save amounts of money that you don't have coming in each month. Remember day-to-day bills take priority over 'some-day' saving. This is why My System must be itemised to gain the full potential of a manageable plan that cannot go wrong..

The prime example of some -day saving is a holiday. You may not be able to go on annual holidays for a year or two, so therefore the amount you calculate when you set up the system should be saved under your holiday subheading account and it will keep on building. What you have saved for your holiday will be the total that you can spend when you take that holiday. So, let me explain exactly how you arrive at the amount you decide to save each month.

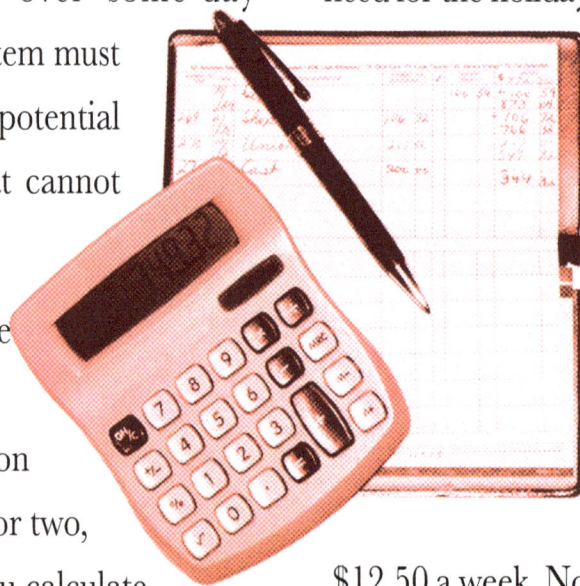

Taking the holiday example again, if you have a holiday plan worked out for the future, take the total costs required to purchase the holiday, including cost of getting to your destination, passport renewal, spending money, everything you will need for the holiday, and then divide by the weeks you have before you will be going on your holiday.

Let's say your holiday and everything else will cost $1,000 and you will be going in about a year and a half's time: so $1,000 divided by say, 80 weeks = $12.50 a week. Now you need to decide to keep back that amount of money, every week for 80 weeks, and not take it to use it for anything else, then you can sit back and WATCH IT GROW. You can go on one big holiday or have smaller holidays like weekends away.

If the price of any of your bills increases, obviously you will need to increase the weekly amount you save ready for the next time that bill comes in.

This may mean for a few weeks the amount saved is actually lower than it should be, but if you divide the total increase by the remaining weeks until payment is due, you can add that amount to what you're already saving, and you will be able to catch up with the payments by the time the next bill is due. Show a negative on your paperwork only until you catch up. Once a bill has been paid, revise the total amount due and keep your savings at the new higher rate as long as required.

This way you will keep on top of price increases.

Why Not Just Bank The Amount Needed Each Week Without Keeping A Record?

A. Simply, so you know all essential bills will be covered within the time required.

B. To stop you thinking you have money in the bank to spend when you don't!

C. To help you to live within your means.

D. And most importantly, you can live life stress-free knowing you have all your incoming bills covered. That's a great feeling!

E. Whenever necessary you can add, remove or change any part of the system

Take the worry and pressure off

We all know bills keep coming in. At one time or another, I'm sure we have all heard other people say, and even have said these things ourselves:

"The rates and insurance bills on the house are due!"
"The car registration is due!"
"Where am I going to find the money for that?"

So what, I might ask! We all knew those bills were coming! It shouldn't come as a surprise to any of us when a bill arrives at our door.

But if you implement this simple system, you will be able to relax, knowing you've got it all covered. And the great thing is, the system will actually help you save a ton of money over the years.

Follow My System, and you will never have to worry about that again.

Please Note:

In My System, we are not including mortgage/rental payments, food, petrol, cigarettes, alcohol, or other weekly sundries.

These are everyday living costs which you need to cover **on top** of all the incoming bills that will be in Your System. These two totals, when added together, will show you what payday-income you need to have to cover your lifestyle. If your every day living expenses plus the cost of your incoming bills is more than your total income, then you are living beyond your means and will need to make adjustments.

This is called Budgeting. You will find an example sheet of a budget on the last page. Use it to fill in as much detail as you can about what you have coming into your household each payday, whether weekly, fortnightly or monthly, and calculate what your outgoings in terms of essential everyday expenditure and expected bills will be.

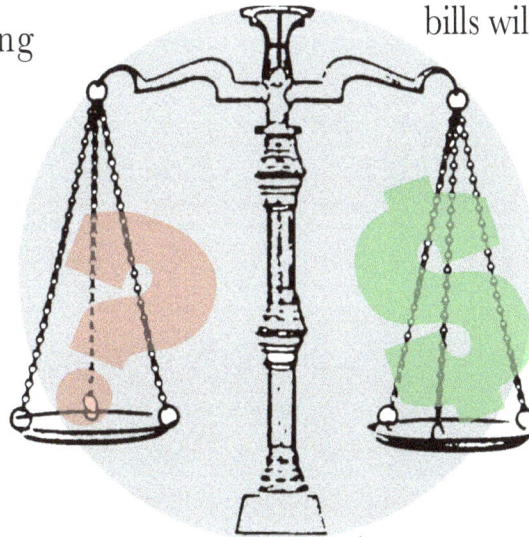

It can take up to 12 Months to put My System into place but only one payday to start seeing the benefits of converting My System into Your System. But essentially the time-frame to implement this is up to you, you have to go at your own pace and make changes as and when you are ready. Unless you have the total money to cover the annual costs of all your bills saved in advance, which none of us ever has, you will normally need to allow a full twelve months for My System to turn over on all the utility/loan accounts that you require for your household.

But because you will be introducing one bill at a time, you will not feel the pinch too badly.

With patience and the guidance of this book, Your System will start working for you immediately.

It's easy! When your first bill arrives, you pay it -then create a subsection in your folder or on your spreadsheet with the calculations worked out as per the example below. The first payday after you have paid up-to-date, you can then start putting away the weekly amount you have calculated ready for the next time that bill becomes due. As the bills all arrive at different times, you pay each one up-to-date then start your weekly payment for that new item into the Your System account. Always remember not to use the money in this account for any other purpose than paying the bills on your list. You will need to exercise self-control.

So in the beginning you may only be paying $30 a week into the Your System account but this amount will increase as each bill is cleared and you add each one onto your list under its heading. When Your System is completed and you are happy with your entries, this will then become the total amount to be paid each payday into the Your System account.

If you have payments automatically deducted from your account, for example direct debits, you can continue with this type of payment but you need to remember to allow for these payments in Your System in the same way as those you settle quarterly etc in one lump. But just leave that payment in your regular account before moving Your System's dollar amount to your elected account or position on the list as discussed earlier. Before you know it, over a period of 12 months you will have the whole system in place.

You will never have to worry about having the money for your bills again. For a very small outlay you can have Your System on track. Requirements: 5 very simple tools needed

Method:

1. *A4 Folder*
2. *Paper*
3. *Subject-Dividers*
4. *Calculator, and lastly…*
5. *…Patience!*

As you put this system into practice, you will see Your System start to grow, and you will be amazed how easy it is for you to budget successfully with this proven method.

As I am not a qualified financial advisor or accountant, the below statements are just suggestions based on many years of putting them into practice and based on my own experiences of what has worked for me and my family.

I would advise you to deposit the money you save for bill payments into a separate account other than your regular bank account(s), even if it means opening up a new account, to avoid the

temptation of spending it or accidentally using the money for other things.

Remember, this money is not for anything apart from the bills it is set up to pay - your bills that you know are coming in. Always tell yourself that the money is already spoken for, that it is not yours to spend, but that it belongs to the utility or loan-company, who will be sending in their bill for it. You might like to consider using this account to help build up your savings record and improve your credit-score rating as the money will acumulate in this account. This will then stand you in good stead should you wish to apply for a loan, mortgage or credit service in the future.

If your mortgage has a redraw facility, or is of the off-set type, you could consider placing all the money from Your System into your home-loan account and when money is required for your incoming bills, use the optional redraw facility.

This could potentially save you thousands of dollars in interest for the life of your mortgage and will help you pay off the home-loan more quickly. Remember to keep a record of how much you have transferred from Your System. You will be able to find this amount by adding up the total balances on each page of Your System in your folder or spreadsheet.

Even if you don't have the redraw option on your mortgage and you have to open a new account, you will still save yourself significant sums of money for the whole life of your loans or bills. If you're not sure if you have a redraw option, just check your home-loan paperwork or ring or visit your branch and ask them to help you.

You can position your incoming due and paid invoices in a plastic sleeve inside your folder behind your calculating page or at the back of your folder. When the next invoice comes in replace with new invoice or keep if you wish. If you set up a kit for yourself you will then experience how well the manual system can work for you. Hands On

The Method

To do your calculations is somewhat time-consuming at the beginning, but once you've set it in place, it is simple and even enjoyable as you see My System start working as Your System!

In My System, I use all the basic annual bills that the average household will need.

If you have anything else to add or to remove from the list, it is as simple as putting a new page in your folder, or taking an old one out. Add a subdivider for each particular bill, then calculate each one out the same as all the other household bills that you will incur. You can have as many divided subheadings or subsections as you wish, as long as your income can accommodate Your System.

In Your System, you save payments for what is applicable to you.

I would even recommend going so far as to create a named subdivider with your name on it, and a separate one for your partner, to save for your hobbies, music, or other interests, especially if these are a regular part of your expenditure. Every dollar counts. Imagine thinking to yourself, "Wow, I love those shoes!" Then thinking, how much do I have under my name? You might

look in the subdivider with your name on it and find you have more than enough for a splurge.

If not, you can take heart that it won't be long before you can really go out and treat yourself - with no feelings of guilt or wondering how you will pay the bill when it comes in or whether you need to keep what you've spent a secret as you couldn't really afford it. That is just one small example.

Then, if you decide to go ahead and buy those amazing shoes, you could put them on your credit card, get the points, transfer the money to credit card immediately, so therefore the points system is also put to work on your behalf.

If you can pay bills annually once My System is set up, leave the money in your account to increase the interest you receive on it. It is also worth bearing in mind that sometimes there is a discount on paying annual payments in one lump, so again you'll be gaining both ways-a reduction on your bill amount, and interest on the money you've saved towards the next bill payment.

Always ensure that what you put onto your credit cards can be paid off before the interest period begins. I have never paid interest on my credit card because of My System.

Easy steps to implementing your system

Step One

Collect all your bill invoices and sit down when you have plenty of time. Get a coffee or cup of tea. I really want you to enjoy this as you are in control. You can feel empowered as you move along, setting up your system to suit you. This is not a punishment or a dreary chore.

Step Two

Write each name on a subdivider - for example, RATES – and insert into folder with a blank piece of paper behind it. On top of your blank sheet, do as per example below: RATES $2,000 p.a. DIVIDED x 52 = $38.46 per week. Round up to nearest dollar: $39

$$\$2,000 : 52 = \$38.46$$

Move onto next invoice and next divider, and continue in this way until all are inserted.

If you pay quarterly and have just paid a quarter, still calculate out by 52 and the money will still be there when the next bill comes in.

Step Three

After calculating all your bills as shown above, add them all up and this will give you the weekly total to cover those incoming bills that you need to put away weekly or fortnightly or monthly depending on your pay structure.

Above all, don't panic when you get the end result – we have not finished yet!

Step Four

I do this on the front inside cover of my folder every week as things often change. Now that covers your bills. What about your weekly living expenses?

Calculated out for 2 persons:

(Although remember all our requirements are different, so you may have different to-tals to mine, these are just an example to show you.)

FOOD   = $150
PETROL/GAS   = $50

LOAN   = $40
CASH ALLOWANCE   = $40 ($20 each)
MORTGAGE/RENT   = $300
CIGARETTES/DRINKS,
not added with food total   = $50

Step Five

You can position your incoming due and paid invoices in a plastic sleeve inside your folder behind your calculating page or at the back of your folder. When the next invoice arrives replace old invoice with the new invoice.

All of the above money has to be found.

Total above is $630 which, when added to Your System weekly savings amounts, let's say $346 for the sake of an example, equals a total of $976 minimum needed every week! Remember no one else can see how you are going to spend your money. It's all yours!

If you do not match outgoings with income you need to re-evaluate your lifestyle so you can live without financial stress and stay within your budget.

The above is a sample only, full example is on last page

Due to price increases, your totals will change regularly and this will help you see how much everyday-living is costing you and then you can do some research and possibly find a less expensive company. This is particularly true of insurance agencies, media companies and power companies.

If you prefer something a little more high-tech, you can do all of the above on a spreadsheet in Excel. Instead of subdividers, you will simply create a new page within your spreadsheet for each bill or item you are adding to Your System. You will probably know that you can add a name to each tab at the bottom of the page, and can colour-code the tab too if you want to. You can also insert a simple formula to add up the amounts every time you put a new payment on the page, and can even have a front sheet which will show the separate and collective total for the amounts in Your System and again as with the paper system, you can highlight these totals. However, it's always good to have a paper back-up in case your electricity goes off the day you want to check something!

Another way My System can work for you is that by paying yourself an allowance, you will always have a little cash in your purse so you won't feel deprived or resentful at having to put all your money into Your System. You should have allowed for what you spend your money on in terms of necessary items so the cash allowance will be for extras and unexpected items. As always, though, if it is not working, take some time to re-evaluate.

You must stay in control of your finances, or they will control you. You can only spend what you have. Be honest with yourself because bad debit will catch up to you.

Change your system to suit your specific needs or it will not work!

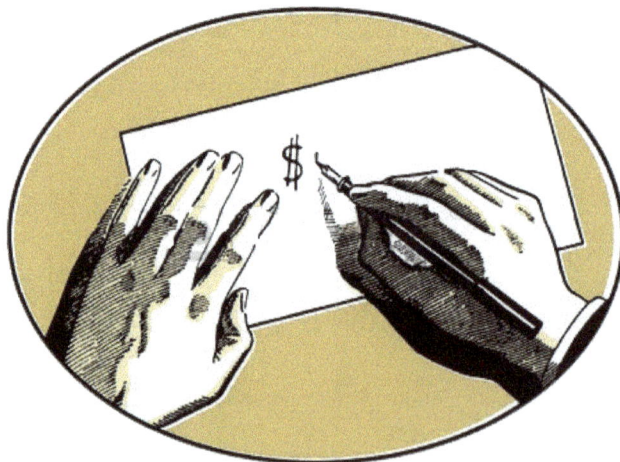

It is all in Your Control!

Your income is your business. To turn My System into Your System, simply adjust your outgoings and requirements according to your income and the bills you need to meet each payday.

This will put You in Control!

Remember, it may be tough in the beginning. You may need to learn to really stick to what you've calculated you need to do, and it will be tough on occasion to say no to spur-of-the-moment wants and needs, however tempting the sales pitch!

But you will be amazed at the difference it will make to your life. You will never have to worry about incoming bills again.

You may not avoid debt altogether but you will learn the value of money, and the best way to make use of it. And think how much money you will save over ten years or even twenty on your home-loans, credit cards and expenditure! Pass this system on to your kids and watch them live without stress and money worries.

Thanks for reading my book! It is now up to you to put into practice the guidelines I recommend. All I can say is, My System has never let me down, nor anyone else who has followed it.

Thinking of you all out there!

Good Luck!

Electricity Bill Example

This example is how you set up your system, it will suit all of your bills and you should apply this example to all your bills and expenditure per page. Review each bill as it comes in to make sure all of your numbers are correct and adjust if you find you are running at a minus for too long -the balance is what you have to put into your system.

THIS IS A QUARTERLY PAYMENT GUIDE

DATE	AMOUNT BANKED	BALANCE	DATE	AMOUNT BANKED	BALANCE
WEEK 1	$ 39.00	$ 39.00			
WEEK 2	$ 39.00	$ 78.00			
WEEK 3	$ 39.00	$ 117.00			
WEEK 4	$ 39.00	$ 156.00			
WEEK 5	$ 39.00	$ 195.00			
WEEK 6	$ 39.00	$ 234.00			
WEEK 7	$ 39.00	$ 273.00			
WEEK 8	$ 39.00	$ 312.00			
WEEK 9	$ 39.00	$ 351.00			
WEEK 10	$ 39.00	$ 390.00			
WEEK 11	$ 39.00	$ 429.00			
WEEK 12	$ 39.00	$ 468.00			
June bill amount (Bill comes in)		$ (435.00)			
balance carried forward		$ 33.00			
WEEK 1	$ 39.00	$ 72.00			
WEEK 2	$ 39.00	$ 111.00			
WEEK 3	$ 39.00	$ 150.00			
WEEK 4	$ 39.00	$ 189.00			
WEEK 5	$ 39.00	$ 228.00			
WEEK 6	$ 39.00	$ 267.00			
WEEK 7	$ 39.00	$ 306.00			
WEEK 8	$ 39.00	$ 345.00			
WEEK 9	$ 39.00	$ 384.00			
WEEK 10	$ 39.00	$ 423.00			
WEEK 11	$ 39.00	$ 462.00			
WEEK 12	$ 39.00	$ 501.00			
September bill amount (Bill comes in)		$ (595.00)			
balance carried forward		$ (94.00)			

You can run at a minus or make this amount up
If you make up the amount of $94 you will start with $39
The following example runs at a minus

$2000 p.a. divided by 52 = $38.46 a week (round up to $39)

DATE	AMOUNT BANKED	BALANCE	DATE	AMOUNT BANKED	BALANCE
WEEK 1	$ 39.00	$ (55.00)			
WEEK 2	$ 39.00	$ (16.00)			
WEEK 3	$ 39.00	$ 55.00			
WEEK 4	$ 39.00	$ 94.00			
WEEK 5	$ 39.00	$ 133.00			
WEEK 6	$ 39.00	$ 172.00			
WEEK 7	$ 39.00	$ 211.00			
WEEK 8	$ 39.00	$ 250.00			
WEEK 9	$ 39.00	$ 289.00			
WEEK 10	$ 39.00	$ 328.00			
WEEK 11	$ 39.00	$ 367.00			
WEEK 12	$ 39.00	$ 406.00			
December bill amount (bill comes in)		$ (456.00)			
balance carried forward		$ (50.00)			
WEEK 1	$ 39.00	$ (11.00)			
WEEK 2	$ 39.00	$ 28.00			
WEEK 3	$ 39.00	$ 67.00			
WEEK 4	$ 39.00	$ 106.00			
WEEK 5	$ 39.00	$ 145.00			
WEEK 6	$ 39.00	$ 184.00			
WEEK 7	$ 39.00	$ 223.00			
WEEK 8	$ 39.00	$ 262.00			
WEEK 9	$ 39.00	$ 301.00			
WEEK 10	$ 39.00	$ 340.00			
WEEK 11	$ 39.00	$ 379.00			
WEEK 12	$ 39.00	$ 418.00			
March bill amount (bill comes in)		$ (378.00)			
balance carried forward		Plus $40			

Tip: Remember, anything that is your weekly survival gets paid first.

Our Weekly Budget Template

To get the most out of your weekly budget, we've included a template you can use. Write directly in the book and stick at the front of your folder or create your own, print and use.

WEEKLY BUDGET	AMOUNT
This amount is to be taken out of your income immediately No inserts required for the below, these are your survival amounts up front	
	$
	$
	$
	$
	$
	$
	$
	$
	$
Total for the week	$
Inserts are to be done for the below, divide everything by 52 weeks	
	$
	$
	$
	$
	$
	$
	$
	$
	$
Total for the week	$
INCOMING MONEY NEEDED	$

Copyright 2015 © Kathleen Walter

ISBN: 978-1-925846-35-5

Published by Vivid Publishing
A division of Fontaine Publishing Group
P.O. Box 948, Fremantle
Western Australia 6959
www.vividpublishing.com.au

A catalogue record for this
book is available from the
National Library of Australia

www.ingramcontent.com/pod-product-compliance
Lightning Source LLC
Chambersburg PA
CBHW040155200326
41521CB00021B/2612